Copyright © 2019 Noble Necessities, LLC.

by *Tammy R. Nobles*

All Rights Reserved

No part of this book may be reproduced or copied in any form or by any means, electronic, mechanical, photocopying, recording or by any information storage or retrieval system without prior written permission of the Publisher.

All Scripture quotations, unless otherwise noted, are taken from the KING JAMES VERSION (KJV): KING JAMES VERSION, public domain.

Noble Necessities, LLC
http://tammyrnobles.com

Library of Congress Catalog Card Number:
ISBN 978-1-891282-27-0

Published by Million Words Publishing, LLC
www.millionwordspublishing.com

Book designed by Missy Robbs | Graphic Designer + Photographer
www.missyrobbs.com

Printed in the United States of America
First Edition 2019

ACKNOWLEDGMENTS

With God on my side, nothing is impossible—Thank you Father.

A huge thank you with hugs and kisses to my #1 supporter and friend—my mom. Thank you for just being the carefree and loving mom that you are to me. We have gone through a lot and yet together we leap forward. I appreciate all you have done and continue to do for me.

Son of mine, thank you for giving me a reason to push through it all, in spite of it all! Thank you for encouraging me when it can easily be the opposite way around.

*To my biological and adopted family, thank you.
I appreciate you all for believing in me.*

PREFACE

The Noble Life Activity Journal is a compilation of actions and activities that helped guide me to experience a life of freedom. I had to give up negative self-talk, unpack the emotional baggage, and start seeing things differently. This didn't happen overnight, but one day, one step at a time. Now, it's your time to start making daily moves to embrace the life you desire to live through *The Noble Life Activity Journal*.

I am still a work in progress!
Daily I decide to take a step closer to accomplish my goals, dreams, and desires.

Let's flourish together!

#leapforward

This *Noble Life Activity Journal* belongs to:

THE NOBLE LIFE

What's your mindset, mood, and next move?

Whatever it is—everything starts with today!

Right now,
in this very moment,
you have made the decision
to create a mindset and environment of intentional actions.

This is true because you're reading this journal.

The Noble Life Activity Journal is designed to encourage you to take daily steps toward creating a life of consistent wins, through commitment to self, discipline, and targeted actions.

There's no time like today to:

Be Noble

Be Intentional

Be Encouraged

Be the **YOU** the world has been waiting on...

LET'S GO!

#tagin

Mindset is EVERYTHING.

Make today a **NOBLE** day by shifting your mindset.

Today I commit to **ME!**

STOP!!!

Before you continue this journey,
let's take a moment to stop, be honest, and identify roadblocks.

Spend the next 5 minutes or more to identify things that seem to stop you, block you, or hinder you.

THINK ABOUT THE FOLLOWING:

What those things are?

Who those people may be?

What are some of my unhealthy behaviors?

What are my limited beliefs?

_____

What road blocks exist that may prevent me from living a Noble Life?

What behaviors do I exhibit that need to be altered or completely stopped?

Let go of the previous things that no longer serve you in a positive manner.

Stop holding on to old stuff.

Old mindsets.

Old behaviors.

Old thoughts.

Old relationships.

Now, use the next few pages to write them down. Take your time. Use extra pages in the back if necessary (be sure to title the page if you use blank pages).

Identify old things you must release!

_____

_____

_____

_____

_____

_____

_____

_____

_____

_____

_____

_____

Everyday is a **NOBLE** day.

Let's deal with this list!

In a quiet personal space, complete the activity below.

Pull out your list.

Open the palm of the hand you use to write.
It's typically your strongest hand.

Now, use your other hand to place all of the things you identified that stop you, people that block you, things that hinder you—all of your negative self-talk and anything else you listed—call out each of them and place them in the palm of your hand.

Next, call out the things you were reluctant to write.

Ball up your hand as hard as you can and
THROW ALL OF IT OUT!
Out the window. Out the door. In the dumpster—out!
Throw it all out!

Now take three deep, cleansing breaths.
*Breathe in through your nose, hold it briefly,
and then release through your mouth.*

1. Think about where you are in life. What things are you most happy with right now?

   _____

   _____

2. What things would you like to change?

   _____

   _____

3. What projects or goals would you like to accomplish?

   _____

   _____

4. What does life look like when you accomplish the goal or complete the project?

   _____

   _____

5. What things are needed to make them happen?

   _____

   _____

Pause now and just allow yourself time to ponder.
Use the *Activity Chart* on the next page as a starting point.

RIGHT NOW, I AM...

_____

_____

RIGHT NOW, I FEEL...

_____

_____

RIGHT NOW, I AM NOT HAPPY WITH...

_____

_____

RIGHT NOW, THINGS I WANT TO CHANGE ARE...

_____

_____

RIGHT NOW, MY MOST PRESSING PROJECT IS...

_____

_____

My **RIGHT NOW** is contributing to my future to make me stronger, better, and will leverage me to my next!

Mindset is Everything

#makeitaNOBLEday

My past is just that...**PAST.**

I begin making better choices today.

THE DREAM ESCAPE

Let's take a moment to dream. It's important to dream, because dreams help you imagine your destiny subconsciously.

Give yourself permission to *dream* and begin taking steps to move towards your dream target.

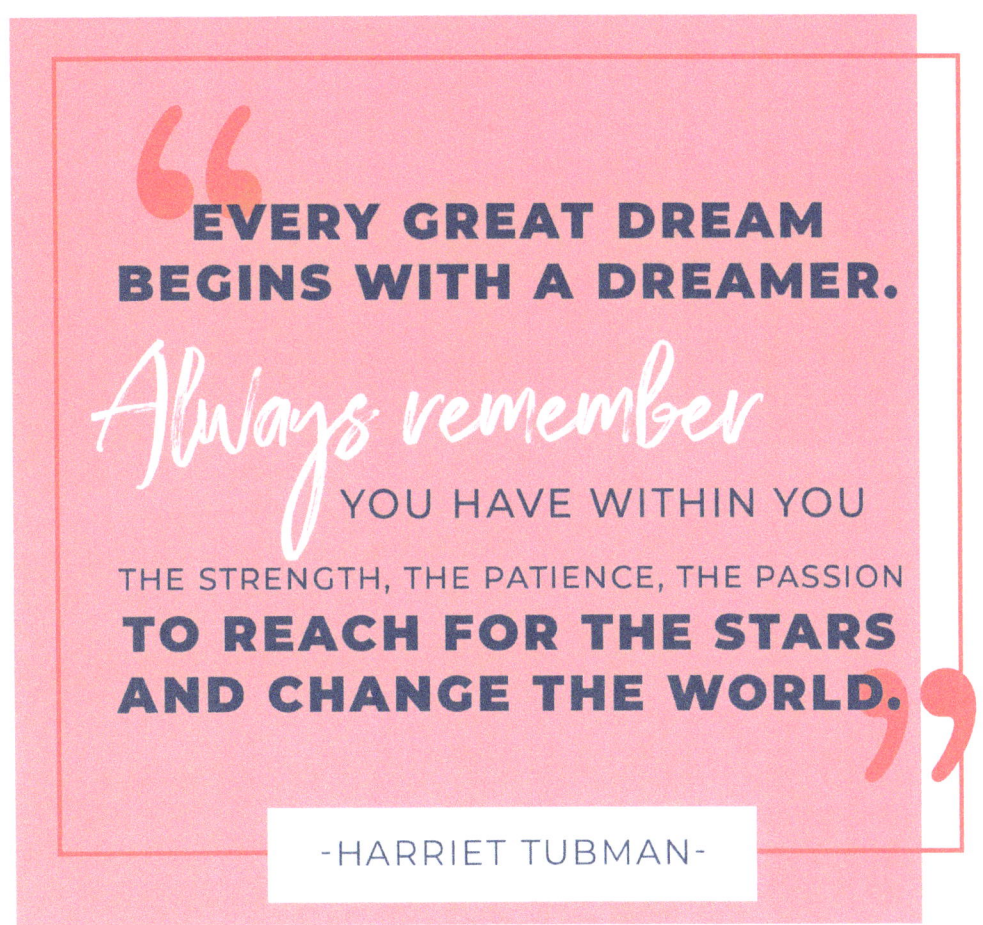
"EVERY GREAT DREAM BEGINS WITH A DREAMER. Always remember YOU HAVE WITHIN YOU THE STRENGTH, THE PATIENCE, THE PASSION TO REACH FOR THE STARS AND CHANGE THE WORLD."

-HARRIET TUBMAN-

DREAMS

_____

_____

_____

_____

_____

_____

_____

_____

_____

_____

Keep on **DREAMING!**

#makeitaNOBLEday

My future is bigger, better, and brighter.

DREAMS
LEAD TO *visions.*

VISIONS
LEAD TO *goals.*

GOALS
LEAD TO *action.*

ACTION
LEADS TO *success!*

#makeitaNOBLEday

WRITE THE VISION

Take the time to write your vision. Use your dreams to write your vision. Dreams typically occur subconsciously while vision occurs consciously.

Now that you see it, let's write the vision so it becomes clear.

What are some of the things you see yourself accomplishing this month?
In 6 months? By the end of this year? 5 years from now?

What things will you learn?

What do you envision accomplishing?

What does that look like when you accomplish them?

Describe it here:

Today I show up to win.

VISION IS EVERYTHING.

Use the next few pages to draw, write, or cut out pictures to place in your mini vision board. A vision board is important because it provides a picture of your vision. Place things on the board that represent your vision.

Once you're done, take a picture of your board and put it in a space you frequent often. Spend time viewing your board. Take time to write goals for you to accomplish the things on the board and take note of the manifestation.

This is your season to soar!

#makeitaNOBLEday

"Where there is no vision, the people perish…"
-Proverbs 29:18

Declare the vision by writing declarations about your vision. Use positive statements beginning with things like I will, I am, I declare, etc.

___

___

___

___

___

___

___

___

___

___

___

___

I am committed to the process.

INTENTIONALITIES

Make today count!

Be intentional with your time and your actions.

Stop procrastinating.

Do it **NOW!**

Stop avoiding hard decisions.

Stop with the bad habits.

Stop putting off your dreams, your business, and your future.

Start today!

Be intentional.

1. What are some of the things you have put off to avoid doing or dealing with?

   a.

   b.

   c.

   d.

   e.

   f.

2. Ask yourself why you are avoiding them.

3. Be intentional today. Pick one and do it!

Be intentional daily.

Then repeat it.

Stop smothering your dreams!

Be intentional.

Allow yourself to be the great **YOU** that you are designed to be today!

Being committed to the process doesn't always feel good, but it's necessary.

Declaration

Today, I make daily choices that lead to my dreams becoming a reality.

In an effort of living an intentional life, it's important to have daily habits. Creating daily habits establishes standards and will help you focus and stay on target.

Below is a list of a few daily habits:

- Pray
- Tell certain people "I Love You"
- Career time
- Business time
- Self-care time
- Workout
- Meditate

DREAM REMINDER

Neatly write the dream you will intentionally focus on accomplishing first.

Post it! See it! Say it! DAILY.

Make noble moves daily towards your dreams.

Take a moment to create your **CURRENT** list of daily habits. Then, use the next page to create a list of things you would like to add to your daily habits. Be sure to add habits that will help you take daily steps towards your dreams, projects, or goals.

_____

_____

_____

_____

_____

_____

- -

- -

- -

Use the *Change Chart* space below to identify daily habits:

CURRENT HABITS	HABITS TO ADD

Change happens when I decide to take action and make changes!

#makeitaNOBLEday

I am moving out of my own way.

Today is the beginning of my new beginning.

LET'S TAKE A LOOK

Take a bird's-eye view to look inside you, around you, above, and behind you!

Now let's look at some of the things you've already overcome...

Imagining your future is just as important as reflecting about your past. This is imperative because it helps you build self-awareness.

When you are aware of who you are, what your personal standards are, and what things are important to you, it will help you gain clarity and understanding of your emotions and thrive factors.

Make a list of your **WINS**...things you have overcome!

This is your **VICTORY LIST!**

I AM MORE THAN A CONQUEROR.

I make a difference.

I'M UNSTOPPABLE.

I'M UNBREAKABLE.

Today, I am allowing myself to feel, heal, and grow.

Take a moment to appreciate all the amazing things about you.

Use the list below to describe you, your character, and things that make you unique by using the alphabet. Each word or words should begin with the designated letter.

a. _____   n. _____

b. _____   o. _____

c. _____   p. _____

d. _____   q. _____

e. _____   r. _____

f. _____   s. _____

g. _____   t. _____

h. _____   u. _____

i. _____   v. _____

j. _____   w. _____

k. _____   x. _____

l. _____   y. _____

m. _____   z. _____

LISTEN

It's okay to be silent. You don't need to always have all the answers.

You don't have to know every next step.

You **DO** have to listen.

Listening is an empowering skillset that helps you communicate effectively.

Listen to your inner voice.

Listen to things and people that influence you positively.

Effective listening skills help build better relationships, allow you to be present in the moment, and understand people better. These skills also allow you to be silent to receive guidance.

What are you listening to? Who are you allowing to influence you?

STOP. LOOK. LISTEN.

-Make Today A Noble Day-

NOBLE THOUGHTS TO PONDER:

- » Nothing in life is perfect.
- » You can overcome any obstacle.
- » Seek help.
- » Be positive.
- » Prepare to function outside your normal comfort zone.

I am willing to fight for my wins—I deserve it.

Boss up!

Be
On
Self
Success

I challenge myself to be better.

I refuse to lose...even when I fail.

PERSONAL MISSION STATEMENT

Mission statements define a _____ .

Knowing who you are, understanding your passion, strengths, gifts, challenges, talents, and your abilities, all aid you in being free to live your best, overflowing, victorious life.

You have purpose! It's your personal mission to fulfill your purpose. Use the steps below to help guide you in crafting a personal mission statement.

Be authentic and honest. Take your time!

Typically, mission statements are connected to businesses. Mission statements define who a business is, their purpose, and help them create vision for the company's future.

The same reasons a company needs a mission statement are the same reasons you need a personal mission statement. After all, you are the Chief Executive Officer of your life! You are the person in the driver's seat, making decisions, creating relationships, and developing future plans.

BOSS UP!

Let's take some time to create your personal mission statement. **Your personal mission should be one or two statements that include the following:**

1. What you like to do.
2. How you operate.
3. Why you want to excel.

Example:

DISCIPLINE

Discipline is a code of behavior.

Having a life of discipline leads to a life of success!
Please see the **21-Day Journal** to help you change negative habits.

What's at the center of your interest or activity today?

Distraction will not move me out of position.

Focus on your commitment, not your feelings.

Today, I will focus on _____

DON'T BE HELD CAPTIVE!

Don't allow yourself to be a prisoner to your own thoughts!

Say these out loud today!

DON'T DIE IN THE MOMENT!

When life happens—let it! Allow yourself to be in the space you are! Give yourself permission to feel, cry, and deal with things your own way.

However, you can't take residence in that space.

You have so much to give to the rest of the world! Don't allow one mistake, one moment, one thing, to make the rest of the world miss out on all you have to give.

We need you!

DISTRACTIONS

A thing that prevents someone from giving full attention to something else.

- diversions
- interruptions
- disturbances
- interference
- hinderances

Don't allow distractions to move you out of position!

_____

I will not be distracted today.

MONKEY WRENCHES

You are positioned to be successful.

Don't allow monkey wrenches (trials, challenges, mistakes, or mishaps) to move you into a space of giving up. Sometimes monkey wrenches come to wake you up, give you a reality check, help you refocus, or regroup.

Whatever you do, stay in position!

I will not allow monkey wrenches to make me give up.

I will continue to move forward, today!
I will use my monkey wrenches as a tool to develop ground and change.

IT IS POSSIBLE!

All things are possible through Him.

Lean on Him.

Trust in Him.

Take Him at His Word!

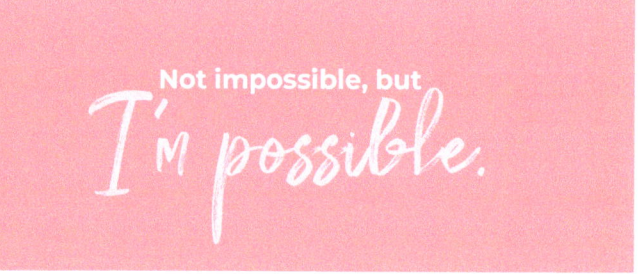

IF YOU DON'T HAVE A PLAN...

you can't expect progress!

SACRIFICE

What are you willing to do today to yield different results?

FAIL FORWARD

"Failure is not an option." A quote I've heard time and time again...but really, who chooses the option to fail?

Think about it. You have a choice to win or lose, but the option selected is failure.

Funny, I know, but when you look at this from a different lens...
NO—failure is not an option, but that doesn't mean I won't experience failure. It simply means, if and when I fail, I will get back up and move forward.

Fail forward!

Don't allow the fear of failure to frighten you from your fabulous future!

Fail forward!

EVALUATE IT!

Are the people in your life helping, hindering, or enhancing you?

> Evaluate it! It may be time to delete or insert people in your life.

SQUAD UP

A squad is a small group of people having a particular task.
Don't walk this journey alone! Who is on your squad?

Identify your success teammates!

» **THE CHEERLEADER:** Celebrates you through it all

» **THE PUSHER:** Accountability partner

» **REALITY-CHECKER:** Gives honest, constructive feedback

» **THE ADVISOR:** Provides sound wisdom

» **THE ACCOUNTABILITY PARTNER:** Holds your feet to the fire

» **THE CONFIDANT:** Trust with sensitive information

» **THE FIGHTER:** Walk by your side through the good, the great, and the bad

» **THE INSPIRATIONAL ONE:** Provides inspiration and encouragement

» **VISIONARIAN:** Helps you to see the big picture

» **THE COACH:** Helps you yield and achieve goals while providing direction and insight

Whose squad are you on?

What role do you play?

Who is missing from your squad?

Great squads know and understand that they need each other in order to be successful and remain great!

GRATEFULNESS

Often in life, we don't always receive what we want, but we get what we need! Have a heart of gratefulness. Some people don't have the privilege of having the want or needs.

What are the top ten things you are most grateful for and why?

I'm grateful for…	because…

In **ALL** things, give thanks.

DON'T FORFEIT YOUR PEACE

A songwriter once said, "O what peace we often forfeit...All because we do not carry everything to God in prayer."

You can have peace!

Peace in your home.

Peace in your mind.

Peace in your job.

Peace in your relationship.

Father,
we thank you for your peace abiding in our lives today.

RE-EVALUATE THE SPACE & SITUATION

» Where's your focus?

» What may be some of the lessons you are forced to learn?

» Believe, this **WILL NOT** take you out.

» Cast your cares on Him.

» Don't try to walk this journey alone!

» Take one day at a time!

Be resilient.

MY DREAMS
ARE MY
new reality.

REMAIN

grateful.

positive.

peaceful.

www.ingramcontent.com/pod-product-compliance
Lightning Source LLC
Chambersburg PA
CBHW081126080526
44587CB00021B/3760